Text: Neil Coates
Series editor: Tony Bowerman
Photographs: Steve Thompson (www.
sunstormphotography.com), Neil Coates,
Shutterstock, Bigstock

Design: Carl Rogers

© Northern Eye Books Limited 2012

Northern Eye Books
ISBN 978-1-908632-11-1
A CIP catalogue record for this book is available
from the British Library.

www.northerneyebooks.co.uk

Important Advice: The routes described in
this book are undertaken at the reader's own
risk. Walkers should take into account their
level of fitness, wear suitable footwear and
clothing, and carry food and water. It is also
advisable to take the relevant OS map with
you in case you get lost and leave the area
covered by our maps.

Whilst every care has been taken to ensure the
accuracy of the route directions, the publishers
cannot accept responsibility for errors or
omissions, or for changes in the details given.
Nor can the publisher and copyright owners
accept responsibility for any consequences
arising from the use of this book.

If you find any inaccuracies in either the text or
maps, please write or email us at the address
below. Thank you.

First published in 2012 by

Northern Eye Books Limited
Northern Eye Books, Tattenhall, Cheshire CH3 9PX
Email: tony@northerneyebooks.com

For sales enquiries, please call 01928 723 744

Cover: Aysgarth Falls (Walk 1)
by Steve Thompson

Contents

Pennine perfection

Designated in 1954, the **Yorkshire Dales** cover 1,762 square kilometres/680 square miles of the central Pennines. As well as some of Yorkshire's most magnificent landscapes, the National Park also includes a corner of Cumbria, where the secluded Howgill Fells loom over the River Lune. 'Dales' is something of a misnomer, for in addition to the beautiful dales the area incorporates great tracts of wild moorland, the famous 'Three Peaks' and an intriguing industrial heritage.

Over 1,300 miles of rights of way allow walkers to explore all facets of the Park. In addition, almost 110,000 hectares of open access land has opened up endless possibilities for exploring this heady mix of limestone and gritstone scenery. Upwards of 8 million visitors a year enjoy this striking countryside with its picturesque stone villages.

Stainforth Force downstream from the 17th-century packhorse bridge

The Yorkshire Dales' best waterfalls

Geology and the way it has shaped the Dales have created a countryside tailor-made for the development of waterfalls. The gritstone fells and moors gather copious rainfall, which they shed along countless becks and rivers that erode the rock into twisting gills and valleys.

Where localised geological conditions bring together the grits and limestones, differential erosion creates bands of resistant rocks over which the becks plunge as hidden cataracts and waterfalls—often called *forces* in the Yorkshire Dales. Each has its own unique form and atmosphere to discover and explore.

> "At the source of the longest river,
> the voice of the hidden waterfall…
> Not known because not looked for."

T.S. Eliot, *Little Gidding V*

TOP 10 **Walks:** Walks to Waterfalls

EACH OF THE DALES IN THE NATIONAL PARK has its own characteristics, largely determined by length and geology, but all have in common a remarkable suite of waterfalls, forces and cataracts. The ones visited in this book have been selected to offer the widest choice of this largesse, from famous, easily reached village falls to secluded gems in deep gorges, where the effort needed to reach them is amply rewarded by magnificent countryside rambles.

Aysgarth & Cauldron Falls — page 8

Janet's Foss & Gordale Scar — page 14

Catrigg Force — page 20

Wain Wath & Kisdon Forces — page 24

Blue skies mirrored in Cauldron Falls

Aysgarth & Cauldron Falls

The Dales' most beautiful village and England's favourite waterfalls on a walk in glorious Wensleydale

What to expect:
Good paths, tracks and lanes throughout

Distance/time: 7km/ 4½ miles. Allow 2½ hours

Start: West Burton village green

Grid ref: SE 016 865

Ordnance Survey Map: Explorer OL30 Yorkshire Dales: *Northern & Central areas: Wensleydale & Swaledale*

After the walk: The village teashop and the Fox & Hounds Inn, both beside West Burton village green

Walk outline
West Burton, secluded in Walden Dale, is widely recognised as the Dales' prettiest village. This walk from the village green slides past Cauldron Falls before threading across haymeadows and past follies to reach Hestholme Bridge. A largely riverside path traces the River Ure at its liveliest, where it tumbles over sets of limestone steps in a series of spectacular falls near Aysgarth. From the old mill, easy paths lead back to West Burton.

Aysgarth Falls
Anyone familiar with the 1991 film *Robin Hood, Prince of Thieves* will recall the scene where Robin and Little John fought with staves amidst the tumbling falls and shoots of a river. This was filmed at various locations along the Ure's tumultuous passage over the long series of limestone ledges that create Upper, Middle and Lower Force falls here at Aysgarth. A pretty scene in dry weather, the thunderous cataracts come into their own after persistent rain. Hidden in a ravine off West Burton's green is Cauldron Falls, a spectacular cascade once painted by JMW Turner.

Aysgarth church

Early purple orchid

The Walk

1. From the foot of **West Burton's green**, turn right on the short lane signed 'Waterfall'. Immediately upstream is **Cauldron Falls**, plunging into a wooded hollow cut by **Walden Beck**. Cross the **packhorse bridge**, bend right and then sharply left to a handgate out of the woods. Look up-field for the sharp end of the woods ahead, use the handgate into these and turn left for 'Morpeth Gate'. Beyond a redundant handgate out of **Barrack Wood**, the path gradually falls to reach the rough track, **Morpeth Gate**.

2. Turn left to pass the farm complex. Just round the left-bend, take the fingerposted handgate on the right, signed for 'Edgley'. Sight the distant field-centre barn; the path heads through handgates and gap-stiles, passing 100 metres right of this barn along a line of trees. Near the far corner slip through a field-gate by a stone barn; then head up for the gate beside a third barn. Above this bear left along the field-foot path to a handgate. Curl left slightly, advancing along the waymarked footpath

passing well-right of the large Georgian house of **Sorrelsykes Park**.

On the terrace to your right are a number of follies. The most eyecatching is the spired 'Rocket Ship', whilst nearby is the 'Pepperpot'. The latter is said to have been built long after the folly-craze of Georgian times, possibly as a smokehouse for the owners of the Sorrelsykes Estate.

Virtually below the spire, fork left as indicated to a handgate onto a main road.

Summer water: *A hot day below Aysgarth Upper Falls*

3. Turn right and walk for 120 metres to reach an entrance on your left. Use the small handgate here, picking up a field path heading for the rounded clump of trees at the far side. *In the distance, Bolton Castle stands high above Wensleydale.* Use the handgate into **Hestholme Wood**; drop to the main road, turn left and carefully negotiate the bridge over **Bishopdale Beck**.

4. Take the waymarked footpath through a handgate at the start of the driveway for **Hestholme Farm**. The path strikes across the meadow to gain a gap-stile; then becomes a well-used way upstream along the fringe of woods bordering the **River Ure**. To your right a stunning rake of falls marks the lowest of the series of limestone ledges over which the Ure tumbles in its 1 kilometre descent from deep pools above **Aysgarth**.

The path skirts the edge of meadows; the river rumbles below, and occasional breaks in the trees allow glimpses of

Evening glow: *The last rays of the sun illuminate Middle Falls at Aysgarth*

the **Lower and Middle Falls** of the Aysgarth series. Now high above the river, the path passes through a spinney of tall sycamores to emerge in a sloping haymeadow below the imposing **village church at Aysgarth**.

At the church tower turn right; join the stepped path beyond the iron handgate and descend to cross the mill-race at the huge mill here.

Yore Mill *(Yore being an ancient spelling of Ure) was built in 1784 as a cotton mill. Cloth produced here was used to clothe*

Garibaldi's troops during his campaign to unite Italy in the 1860s, whilst balaclavas were made for Allied forces during the Crimean War.

Cross the bridge and go immediately left to reach the nearby riverbank at the head of the **Upper Falls** here. *Long a favoured beauty spot, Dorothy Wordsworth was disappointed and wrote, in 1802, 'There was too much water in the river for the beauty of the falls'.*

5. Return to the church tower and go ahead between the low, pollarded lime trees. At the main road cross straight over into a path signed for 'Eshington

Bridge'. A series of six stiles and handgates reaches **Eshington Bridge**.

6. Cross the bridge and in 75 metres turn right on the field path for 'West Burton'. Several pastures take this well-used path past a lonely barn to reach the main road below cottages at **West Burton**. Climb the steps opposite and turn right to the village centre to complete the walk. ♦

Railways and rubbernecks

Aysgarth boomed in Victorian times after the railway reached the village in 1878. Visitors flocked to view the local natural wonders lauded by Wordsworth and Ruskin. Aysgarth Station closed in 1954, although the line to the east survived as a freight line. Today the private heritage Wensleydale Railway runs services from nearby Redmire to Bedale; there are long-term plans to extend the line back through Aysgarth.

Waterfall and plunge pool at Gordale Scar

Janet's Foss & Gordale Scar

To a fairy queen's hidden home and an astonishing waterfall-strewn gorge near Malham

What to expect:
Decent paths, with a challenging scramble; some mud, long flight of steps down

Distance/time: 11km/ 7 miles. Allow 3½-4 hours

Start/finish: Malham pay and display car park

Grid ref: SD 900 626

Ordnance Survey Map: Explorer OL2 Yorkshire Dales: *Southern & Western areas: Whernside, Ingleborough & Pen-y-ghent*

After the walk: Cafés and inns in Malham

Walk outline

From Malham a path curls to reach Janet's Foss waterfall. Above here the walk enters the incredible Gordale Scar, a massive gash in the limestone plateau. Waterfalls tumble down this geological marvel; the walk up beside them is a challenging, if short, scramble up natural steps. Gaining the plateau, the route then follows the Pennine Way past Malham Tarn back to Malham via the inspiring Malham Cove.
Note: Use the 'Round About' route after heavy rain.

Malham

The area around Malham contains amongst the most famous geological features in England, all of which owe their existence to running water. Early in the walk, the lovely Janet's Foss tumbles over a band of tufa rock. Continuing upstream, Gordale Beck debouches from the stunning cleft of Gordale Scar, at the heart of which waterfalls tumble over 30 metres between towering cliffs. Escaping (or avoiding) this spectacular gulch, the walk strikes to Malham Tarn before descending Watlowes, the dry riverbed above mighty Malham Cove, a vast limestone amphitheatre created by a waterfall over 60,000 years ago.

Gordale cataract

Wild rock dove, Malham

The Walk

1. In **Malham** village centre locate **The Smithy**, cross the footbridge and turn downstream beside **Malham Beck**. At the bend turn left for 'Janet's Foss', passing left of **Mires Barn** on a good path beside **Gordale Beck**. This reaches the woodland falls at **Janet's Foss**. *Behind the waterfall here is a cave where, folklore has it, Jennet, the queen of the local fairies lives.*

2. Continue to the nearby lane and turn right to **Gordale Bridge (The 'Round About' starts here)**. Just round the bend turn left along the campsite road. The path soon becomes enclosed by the towering cliffs of **Gordale Scar**, reaching a point where the path fails at a rock band and waterfalls. In good conditions there's a short, testing scramble up the bulbous rock just left of the lower falls; plenty of handholds make this a breeze.

[**Round About:** If the way looks wet or too daunting, retrace your steps to **Gordale Bridge** and take the path signed for 'Malham Cove'. Walk this to the first handgate; from here turn back-right, go through a bush-side higher handgate (Access Land boundary marker) and up the steep slope on a wide grassy path half-right, skirting between the top of **New Cross Knotts** (left) and the gorge of **Gordale Scar**. Trace the good path beside the tumbled wall before meeting the main path out of the Scar at a stone step-stile (**3.**).]

Map scale: 0 — 1km — 1 mile

Deep in the woods: *The braided cataracts of Janet's Foss after rain*

Beyond this rock band the path eases up natural steps to the left of the higher falls; then develops into a path that soon peels up away from the shallowing gorge. Within yards the 'Circumspect' path joins from the left.

3. Keep ahead on the good path over the stile ('Malham Tarn 2m') and then across the grassy uplands through an area of **limestone pavement**.

4. In 1 kilometre this path meets a tarred lane at a stile 130 metres beyond the lone laneside tree; turn right and walk to a cross-lane. Keep ahead on the rougher track signed 'No Cars'; when you can see the lake, head towards its lefthand-edge to reach a corner of **Malham Tarn**.

This is the largest lake in The Dales and also a claimant to the accolade of being the highest natural lake in England. It lies on an upwelling of impervious slate, preventing the water from sinking into the limestone, and is held back by a glacial moraine, or bank of debris, created 11,000 years ago as the ice sheets retreated.

Mighty Malham: *Dramatic storm light illuminates Malham's limestone cliffs*

5. Follow the wide path left to a car park and lane. Go right; just past the wall turn left on the **Pennine Way**. This well-tramped route joins the line of a wall near water sinks where the beck draining Malham Tarn disappears into limestone fissures.

This flows deep underground and re-emerges not below Malham Cove but, rather, south of Malham village at Aire Head Springs.

The path drops into a cleft, bends right, then sharp-left to drop into the deep dry valley of **Watlowes**. In immediate post-glacial times this was formed by a larger river overflowing from a much larger Malham Tarn. This memorable scar in the landscape culminates in the spectacle of **Malham Cove**'s immense cliff.

A waterfall to rival Niagara Falls once plunged over the edge here. Formed by meltwaters from the vast icesheets smothering Northern England 60,000 years ago, these floods took advantage of a geological weakness, the Craven Fault, and cut back deep into the limestone plateau to create today's natural amphitheatre. Take time to explore the remarkable

limestone pavement here. It's treacherous underfoot; but your diligence is rewarded by the remarkable plant and wildflower-rich micro-landscape contained within the deep fissures, or grykes.

6. Facing the panoramic views off the cliff edge, head right to the waymarked footpath down steps. From the bottom a wide path heads back to **Malham** village to complete the walk. ♦

Peregrine falcons

The world's fastest flying birds nest at Malham Cove, where peregrines have reared broods on the cliffs since returning in 1993. Normally hatching in May, the juvenile birds fledge during June: the ideal time to view these raptors. Peregrines have been recorded reaching speeds close to 200mph when 'stooping', or diving, to catch prey on the wing. Look for the National Park peregrine viewing point at the Cove foot between April and July.

Catrigg Force

Catrigg Force

*A grand mix of waterfalls, moorland and valley pastures
beside the river Ribble*

What to expect:
*Paths, lanes and tracks;
muddy and slippery
after rain*

Distance/time: 8km/ 5 miles. Allow 2½-3 hours

Start/finish: Stainforth village car park (pay & display)

Grid ref: SD 820 673

Ordnance Survey Map: Explorer OL2 Yorkshire Dales: *Southern &
Western areas: Whernside, Ingleborough & Pen-y-ghent*

After the walk: The Craven Heifer Inn at the village centre; or
Taitlands Coach House Tearoom just south of Stainforth.

Walk outline

*A walled track rises from Stainforth, levelling at the moorland
edge where a side path slips to the top of Catrigg Force. A
stepped path nearby drops into the chasm and another
notable waterfall. Gaining the plateau, moorland tracks and
lanes open out notable views across the southern Dales before
reaching tiny Langcliffe. Joining the bank of the River Ribble, a
wildflower-rich route leads to the multi-level Stainforth Force,
just outside the village.*

Catrigg Force

Stainforth is swiftly left behind in the valley of the River
Ribble as an ancient track weaves through limestone
pastureland to reach the top end of a deep gorge cut into
the moor by Stainforth Beck. Catrigg Force plummets into
this chasm, falling in two memorable stages through an
echoing, pine-clad cleft enjoyed more than once by the
composer Edward Elgar. Circling back on tracks and lanes,
superb views to Pen-y-Ghent's shapely peak detain before
the Ribble Way footpath is picked up below Langcliffe. A
lovely walk upstream gains the vigorous Stainforth Force,
tumbling below a graceful packhorse bridge.

Stainforth Force

Buttercups

The Walk

1. Turn right from the car park and bend right to cross the bridge over **Stainforth Beck**, beside the village inn. Slip left through the bridge-end gap onto a good path above the beck. Upon meeting a lane, at metal bollards, turn left to the little sloping green here at the head of the village. Bear right; the tarmacked lane soon becomes a rough walled track—the 'Pennine Bridleway'—up the steepening flank of the fellside.

The track ends at a gate into moorland. Use the hand gate on your left, a short path meanders to the top of **Catrigg Force**. Take care here here as the drops are unfenced. **Stainforth Beck** plummets 50 feet before swirling ahead to tumble over another rocky ledge. To reach this use the hand gate off the access path to a wide, ledged area between the falls.

2. Return to use the moor gate and turn right along the wide track to another gate. Just past this, turn right on a green track to reach **Higher Winskill Farm**. Turn left along the surfaced lane, looking back for sublime views to Pen-y-Ghent.

3. At the end, turn right to reach **Langcliffe**. *In Victorian times the village green here was overlooked by the 'Naked Woman' inn!*

4. Take the rough lane from the rear of the car park by the village school. Keep right at the fork, walking a further 300 metres to a fingerpost for 'Stainforth'. Go left; then left at the next gates to the main road. Cross the railway before

0   1km

1 mile

Stainforth Force: *Multiple falls plunge over rock steps below a packhorse bridge*

slipping left on the tarmacked lane leading to a weir over the **Ribble**. *The long millpond here once supplied nearby Langcliffe Place Mills, a paper-mill on the site of a textile mill built in the 1780s.*

5. Cross the weir-foot footbridge and turn right along the riverbank, presently passing opposite another ruinous mill before reaching the edge of a caravan park. Beyond are the lovely multiple falls of **Stainforth Force**, above which is a graceful packhorse bridge (*dated 1675*). Cross this, rise to the main road and turn right to **Stainforth** to complete the walk. ♦

Compose yourself

One visitor who enjoyed this peaceful area was the composer Sir Edward Elgar. To escape his growing celebrity he took to visiting his friend and fellow musician Dr Charles Buck in Settle. From here Elgar regularly explored the byways and paths that led to Catrigg Force, perhaps finding musical inspiration here in the years before The Great War.

Natural pothole at Wain Wath Force

Wain Wath & Kisdon Forces

A surfeit of falls enliven the course of the River Swale through hay meadows between Keld and Muker

What to expect:
Hill tracks, riverside and woodland paths; modest climbs; sheer drops

Distance/time: 12km/ 7½ miles. Allow 4 hours

Start: Keld car park

Grid ref: NY 893 012

Ordnance Survey Map: Explorer OL30 Yorkshire Dales: *Northern & Central areas: Wenseydale & Swaledale*

After the walk: Seasonal café at Keld; Keld Lodge, in Keld, and the Farmers Arms, at Muker, both offer bar meals

Walk outline

The River Swale tumbles from Great Shunner Fell just a couple of miles above Keld's compact village centre. Dashing upstream to Wain Wath Force, this walk then returns on tracks and paths above the Swale to the extraordinary Swinner Gill's hidden falls before threading beside the Swale down to Muker. A farm lane strings along the wooded foot of Kisdon Hill, passing above lively Kisdon Force to return to Keld.

Currack, Cutrake and Kisdon Forces

Tiny Keld stands at the crossways of two of England's most renowned footpaths: the Pennine Way and the Coast-to-Coast Path. It's also arguably waterfall-central, with myriad becks tumbling from the heights to join the upper reaches of the Swale. The rumbling voices of Currack, Cutrake and Kisdon Forces reverberate off the fell-sides and scars, joined by waters crashing down sharp sided valleys like Stonesdale and Swinner Gill. Ancient oak, ash and beech woods cling to the dale-sides here; a swathe of green above the exquisite haymeadows which border the Swale. As counterpoint, the scars of long-gone lead mines add fascination to this sublime landscape.

Swaledale barn

Swaledale ewe

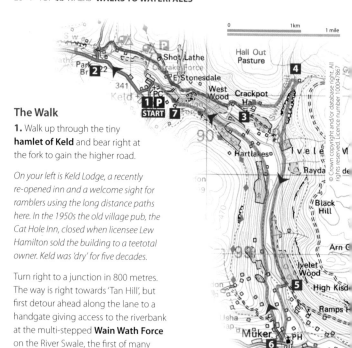

The Walk

1. Walk up through the tiny **hamlet of Keld** and bear right at the fork to gain the higher road.

On your left is Keld Lodge, a recently re-opened inn and a welcome sight for ramblers using the long distance paths here. In the 1950s the old village pub, the Cat Hole Inn, closed when licensee Lew Hamilton sold the building to a teetotal owner. Keld was 'dry' for five decades.

Turn right to a junction in 800 metres. The way is right towards 'Tan Hill', but first detour ahead along the lane to a handgate giving access to the riverbank at the multi-stepped **Wain Wath Force** on the River Swale, the first of many waterfalls on this walk.

2. Take the Tan Hill road across the bridge and around a hairpin bend. Slip right off the next bend down a gated bridleway for 'Ivelet Side and Tan Hill'. This curls round just above the higher of the string of hidden falls above **Currack Force**, continuing then as a firm farm lane to **East Stonesdale Farm**. Join the **Pennine Way** downhill, soon keeping left at a fork and leaving the Pennine Way, instead circling above the vigorous **East Gill Force** at **Stonesdale**. The track rises to a gate before levelling to skirt the top of fine birch woods which smother the deep gorge hiding **Kisdon Force**. Leaving the woods, spring bluebells smother the slopes near an old barn at a sharp bend.

World of swirl: *Frescoes of foam fan out below Wain Wath falls*

3. Just past a longstanding rambler's waymark—an old tractor seat—fork left up the rising track, shortly reaching the dour ruins at **Crackpot Hall**.

This was built in early Elizabethan days as a hunting lodge for local bigwig Lord Wharton, later becoming offices for the local lead mines and a farm, before being abandoned in 1951 due to mining subsidence. Crackpot is held to mean 'hole where crows live'.

Head for the higher building; remaining on the track beyond, which presently reaches a gate through a wall high above the immense canyon of **Swinner Gill**. Once through the gate the path thins considerably. The Gill cleaves a huge gash into the wilderness of East Stonesdale's grouse moors; the ledged path strikes up to the point **High Hole Beck** and **East Grain** meet, marked by a waterfall and nearby old lead-mine workings.

4. Don't cross the stream; rather turn back-right on the path signed for

Swaledale view: *Stone houses dot Swaledale's iconic drystone-walled pastures*

'Muker', walking back down the western side of the Gill on a lower path. This is narrow, steep and occasionally stepped; a challenging route with the reward of descending into this extraordinary waterfall-riven ravine. Crossing the beck, the path rises before bursting out of the narrows to join a wide track heading left down the trough-like **valley of the Swale**, dropping to the river.

5. In 2 kilometres, cross the footbridge and turn right to a nearby fingerposted handgate for Muker. The paved path passes through a series of internationally-renowned wildflower haymeadows, reaching **Muker** at a postbox. Keep ahead to this former lead-mining community, a most attractive village beside **Straw Beck**.

6. Return to the postbox and slip left; then right up a narrow tarred lane signed as a footpath for 'Keld'. At the sharp-lefthand bend bear right through a gate into a walled track. Remain with this, presently dropping to the riverside. Before a tall, lone ash tree, keep left on the walked path away from the Swale through fallen walls, passing ruined barns before rising towards

the woodside, passing near a derelict cottage to enter the woods.

7. Near the end of the woods look for a gap-stile on the right. Confident walkers can take the steep there-and-back path from here down to the powerful **Kisdon Force** falls deep in the gorge. The main route continues high above the river to return to **Keld**, to complete the walk. ♦

Two long-distance trails

The Pennine Way was established in 1965 as England's first official National Trail; 268 miles from Edale in the Peak District to Kirk Yetholm in the Scottish Borders. In contrast, the unofficial Coast-to-Coast walk, created by the renowned Alfred Wainwright in 1973, is Britain's most popular long distance path. Curiously, the 192 mile route from St Bees Head to Robin Hood's Bay still isn't marked on Ordnance Survey maps!

Falls on Posforth Gill

The Strid & Posforth Gill

Powerful and delicate waterfalls amidst the woodlands of the Bolton Abbey estate

What to expect:
Reasonable paths with some rough moorland walking

Distance/time: 10.5km/ 6½ miles. Allow 3-4 hours

Start: Bolton Abbey Estate Sandholme car park, Cavendish Pavilion (fee payable)

Grid ref: SE 078 552

Ordnance Survey Map: Explorer OL2 Yorkshire Dales: *Southern & Western areas: Whernside, Ingleborough & Pen-y-ghent*

After the walk: Refreshments at The Cavendish Pavilion and Bolton Abbey

Walk outline

The walk accompanies the River Wharfe upstream, passing The Strid, a thundering cataract in a wooded gorge. Beyond the ruins of Barden Tower, a short, steep climb gains the flank of Barden Fell. A heathery traverse finds The Valley of Desolation, a forested cleft in the fellside where becks plummet over a series of memorable falls in Posforth Gill. **No dogs allowed, please. Access Land may also be closed for short periods between August and December.**

The Strid & Posforth Force

The River Wharfe collects numerous tributaries before rushing beneath Barden Bridge. It then gushes through a deep, wooded gorge cut in glacial times through the looming fells. At The Strid the river is constricted into a deep fissure down which the waters boom and swirl over tremendous cataracts, emerging into a vale characterised by islets in the stream. It's here that the side becks draining Barden Moor end their tumultuous drop from the heights. Cleaving a sinuous cleft in the fell-side, their waters tumble over a series of shoots and cascades, culminating in the stunning 50 foot high 'mare's tail' falls of Posforth Force.

Barden Bridge

Bluebells

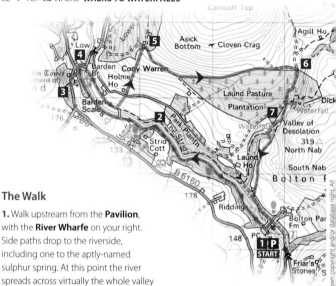

The Walk

1. Walk upstream from the **Pavilion**, with the **River Wharfe** on your right. Side paths drop to the riverside, including one to the aptly-named sulphur spring. At this point the river spreads across virtually the whole valley floor and the exposures of rock reveal folding of the strata. Simply drift with the main track to the point where The Strid is indicated to the right. Take great care in exploring this area, a captivating mix of rushing water, potholed rocks, sudden drops and thick woodland. *The artist JMW Turner completed a watercolour painting of The Strid in 1809.*

2. Beyond **The Strid** the path narrows and climbs high above the lively river; the exposed roots can be slippery here. The way presently descends close to the river again, passing beneath the imposing **Barden Aqueduct**.

This was constructed in the 1850s as part of a complex engineering project to supply water to the rapidly expanding city of Bradford. The waters percolating into the gritstone fells either side of the Wharfe were particularly suited to the washing and bleaching of woollens in the vast mill complexes in Bradford. Tunnels beneath the hills linked reservoirs such as Lower Barden and Grimwith to treatment works at Bingley, near Bradford.

3. The surfaced path shortly reaches **Barden Bridge**. *The current bridge dates*

Still waters: *Foam swirls downstream on the section of the Wharfe called the 'Strid'*

from 1659, built on the site of an earlier crossing that served nearby **Barden Tower**. To view this turn left up the lane.

Barden Tower was built in the fifteenth century for Henry Clifford, a member of the powerful family who controlled great swathes of Northern England. The thickly-walled Pele Tower was built to withstand raids by troops of warring family groups which retained private armies in those feudal times. In Norman times a hunting

lodge stood on the same site. The ruinous tower was another study painted by Turner during his Yorkshire tour. Entry is free.

4. Return to and cross the bridge, turning right through the hand gate immediately at the far end. Walk downstream to the aqueduct and look left for the finger-posted path for 'Coney Warren'. Climb this, using two stiles to reach a lane below a house. Go straight over and up the rough track into Access Land. *The path climbs through boulder-strewn pastures that still shelter rabbits. Coney is another word for rabbit, which*

Green river: *The lovely stretch of the River Wharfe near Bolton Abbey called 'The Strid'*

were once farmed here to provide meat for the Norman lords at Barden.

Continue the gradual climb to a wood-side wall below a building and a fingerpost for **Simon's Seat**.

5. Turn right on the track; in another 70 metres fork right on the muddy track that drops gradually through the heather to meet a lower wall near a wooded corner. Turn left and trace the thin path alongside this wall, outside the woodland. In time the braided path fails; just keep ahead above the wall, shortly picking up a moorland track coming in from your left. Follow this, enjoying fine views across high moorland.

6. At the corner use the handgate, joining a forestry road which meanders down into the woodlands clothing the **Valley of Desolation**. At cross-tracks take the path ahead-left for 'Waterfall Cottage'. As this levels above the beck, divert back-left to view the higher falls in **Posforth Gill**; then return to the main path and continue to a footbridge.

7. Fork right immediately before this onto a narrow path that creeps beside the beck before reaching the top of **Posforth Force**.

The way drops steeply beside the waterfall, continuing across a lower footbridge before climbing out of the gully at grassy pasture. Head ahead-left past the reedy pond, joining a field road which falls via gates to a lane. Turn left; at the cross-lane go right over the wooden bridge back to the **Pavilion** to complete the walk. ♦

'Valley of Desolation'

Hardly a good description of today's verdant vale, the name derives from a catastrophic flood that scoured down the steep gills in 1836, when a massive storm broke over Barden Fell. Records suggest that the little valleys were totally denuded of trees and the boulders that today glow beneath coats of moss and lichen were tossed like marbles from the higher moors. Today, nature has reclaimed most of the scars of the flash flood.

Mill Gill Force

Mill Gill & Whitfield Forces

Two secluded waterfalls and some great views across Wensleydale

What to expect:
paths are uneven in Whitfield Gill, one lengthy ascent

Distance/time: 6km/ 3¾ miles. Allow 2½–3 hours

Start/finish: Askrigg village cross

Grid ref: SD 950 912

Ordnance Survey Map: Explorer OL30 Yorkshire Dales: *Northern & Central areas: Wenselydale & Swaledale*

After the walk: Pubs and tearooms in Askrigg

Walk outline

From Askrigg the walk threads into the wooded Mill Gill and the first secluded waterfall. The way then rises above the beck, continuing until a steep path tempts down into the higher gorge, Whitfield Gill. It's a bit of a scramble to reach the falls where Whitfield Beck cascades over a tree-hung limestone cliff. A stiff climb gains a moor-edge return track with sublime views over Wensleydale.

Mill Gill Force and Whitfield Gill Force

For its size, little Askrigg punches well above its weight. In Georgian times it was an important market town and also a centre for clock-making. JMW Turner visited here in 1816, drawing initial field-sketches of both the waterfalls visited on this walk, although he never put this work onto canvas. He stayed at The Kings Arms Inn, just above the church. This building gained wider fame in the 1970s when, along with other village buildings, it was used as a film location for the BBC television adaptation of James Herriot's *All Creatures Great and Small*—when Askrigg became 'Darrowby'.

Low Straights Lane

Grey wagtail

The Walk

1. From the cobbled square hosting the market cross and old water siphon take **Mill Lane**, to the right of the churchyard. Remain with this winding lane to the edge of the village. Where the lane roughens, slip right on the field path for 'Mill Gill Force'. The path strikes through a buttercup meadow to reach a **derelict old worsted mill**.

The mill launder here carried water to work waterwheels at three mills along the valley. Between them they worked flax, cotton, corn, tweed and woollen cloth—it's said that the socks worn by sailors at Trafalgar were made in Askrigg using yarn produced here.

2. Pass beneath the zinc launder, or trough, and turn right, crossing a footbridge and entering the woodland edge. The path climbs gradually above the dell.

The woods are thick with wood anemones, wild garlic—or ramsons, lesser celandines and bluebells in late spring.

At the waymarked fork keep right for 'Mill Gill Fall only'. The path scurries down into the ravine, shortly reaching the foot of the **Mill Gill Force**. The falls are a recumbent, slightly twisted deluge tumbling from a gaping maw in the limestone cliff above.

3. Return to the fingerpost and turn

Spring flowers: *Lovely but pungent wild garlic in full bloom in Mill Gill woods*

sharply back to the right for 'Whitfield Gill'. At first stay within the woods beside a wall, and later skirt the edge of pasture. Ignore any side paths, always remaining on the track for Whitfield Gill.

At a fork signposted for 'Askrigg via Low Straits', keep left to shortly pass by a barn. In another 100 metres, fork right on a muddy path across decrepit remnants of wooden path-edging. The steepening path falls to the gorge foot

and **Whitfield Gill Force**, a graceful curtain fall over 20 metres high, plunging into a verdant bowl.

Note: The route along the bottom of the gorge is very rocky and may well be impassable after prolonged rain.

4. Head back to the fingerpost and turn sharp-left, shortly crossing a **footbridge** before commencing a long, steady climb out of the gorge. The path, steep in parts, traces a woodland-edge wall separating the deep cleft from moorland-edge pastures.

Wensleydale's best: *Overlooking Askrigg, whose houses cluster around the church*

5. At the top, turn right on the walled track, **Low Straights Lane**.

From the lane, extravagant views stretch down Wensleydale and to the flat-topped Addlebrough Hill. Low Straights Lane was probably created to allow the inclosure of rough moorland two centuries ago. By an Enclosure Award of 1819, the extent of cultivatable land above Askrigg was greatly increased, necessitated in part by food shortages following the Napoleonic Wars. The straight, regular lines of the walls *are indicative of this; older field boundaries closer to the village are much more higgledy-piggledy, reflecting their gradual development over centuries, as opposed to the neat, 'industrial' shapes of the enclosure fields.*

In about a mile you'll pass a small barn on your left, shortly reaching a shallow ford marked by a plank footbridge.

6. Take the gate on the right immediately before this; pass to the left of the barn and strike across the slope above the wooded ravine. Beyond the next barn, cross directly over the walled track, turn left within the pasture and

aim for the large ruined barn in the next field.

Pass right of this to a curving wall; here turn right to find a handgate into a stable-paddock. Slip half-right to another gate and walk through to **Main Street**. Turn left to reach the centre of **Askrigg** to complete the walk. ♦

Early water-powered lights

Below Mill Gill Force a generator house was built in 1910 to house water-powered turbines fed by water from higher up the gorge. This early hydroelectric power enabled nearby Mill Gill House to be the first building in Wensleydale to be lit by electricity. Other buildings were soon wired up. The generator was turned off only when the village was linked to the National Grid in 1949.

Caramel-coloured water courses through Ingleton Glen

Ingleton Waterfalls

One of England's finest waterfall walks below shapely Ingleborough

What to expect:
Well maintained paths, some steep and slippery

Distance/time: 7km/ 4½ miles. Allow 3 hours

Start: Ingleton Falls car park, Ingleton

Grid ref: SD 693 734

Ordnance Survey Map: Explorer OL2 Yorkshire Dales: *Southern & Western areas: Whernside, Ingleborough & Pen-y-ghent*

After the walk: Plenty of inns, cafés and tearooms in Ingleton

Walk outline

A fee is payable to enter the gorges hiding these memorable falls. The outward route joins the River Twiss at Ingleton's fringe. The challenging, steeply-stepped paths thread up wooded Swilla Glen, then past Pecca Falls to Thornton Force before tracing a moorland track around the southern end of Whernside. Beezley Falls start the return beside the River Doe, which separates Whernside from Ingleborough; Rival Falls, Snow Falls and lesser cataracts lead back to Ingleton.

Ingleton Glen

Ingleton Waterfalls

The rivers encountered on this energetic walk are tributaries of the River Lune, which they reach via the River Greta, formed where the Rivers Twiss and Doe meet at the edge of Ingleton. Two of the famous Three Peaks—Whernside and Ingleborough—hang over the town and collect the copious waters which thunder over a series of spectacular falls that have been popular since Victorian tourists flocked to the area by train.

The best time to do this walk is in late spring after heavy rain; not only will the falls be at their most violent but the woods will be bursting with wildflowers.

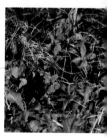

Violets

The Walk

1. The car park is beneath the abutments of an old mineral railway viaduct over the wooded vale. **Ingleton** was once a significant coal-mining centre, whilst quarrying remains an important industry. All thoughts of industry fade as the path narrows above the swirling waters of the **River Twiss**, here named **Swilla Glen**. Throughout the walk the path is often up and down steep steps; it's a challenging route in places. An adventurous section over hanging platforms and beneath yews eases into the well-wooded valley and reaches a sinuous fallen tree.

*The **Money Tree** is crammed full of coins, a practice first started by the Victorians, although most coins seem to be post-decimal. Several other trees and sculptures in the glens are similarly lavishly imbued with coinage.*

Crossing a footbridge, the path reaches a viewing area. Here the gorge sides pull apart, allowing glimpses ahead of the lowest of the multiple **Pecca Falls**. This is scant preparation for the solidly-engineered footbridge and steps that scramble up beside these powerful torrents into **Thornton Glen**, an awesome introduction to the stars of this walk.

2. Well beyond the top fall the way passes by a refreshment cabin, advancing then out of the trees into a wide rocky vale littered with mossy boulders. A

0   1km
½ mile

White mare: *Foaming, peat tinted water plunges over the lip of Thornton Force*

distant rumbling presages arrival at the memorable spectacle of **Thornton Force**, largest of the lot.

The renowned artist JMW Turner sketched the falls on his grand tour in 1816; the scene remains as enchanting today. A vast curtain of water drops 14 metres over a wide semicircle of limestone, tumbling into a deep plunge-pool before swirling over cataracts en-route to Pecca Falls.

Above Thornton another string of limestone steps produce an endless **series of falls** and shoots along the Twiss. Here it flows out of remote **Kingsdale**, secluded between **Whernside** (Yorkshire's highest peak) and **Leck Fell** (Lancashire's highest) with notable limestone cliffs and crags. Crossing a footbridge, the stepped path climbs to join an old, walled packhorse track; turn right along this.

3. The steep slopes to your left are **Twisleton Scar**, the southern end of Whernside's whaleback of a mountain. Past a gate the track becomes tarred;

Spotlit trees: *Late evening light catches the limestone pavement above Ingleton*

keep left at **Twisleton Hall Farm**, passing left of the barns into a field track which falls easily, revealing mouthwatering views across the dale of the **River Doe** to shapely Ingleborough. Cross straight over **Oddie's Lane**, dropping to the Ingleton Scenery Company's property at nearby **Beezley's Farm**.

There's a lovely little diversion through the handgate on the left here. The track falls to a wide ford and stepping stones across the Doe, offering an idyllic view

of Ingleborough's peak, framed by alder and willow beyond a riverbank rich with buttercups and violets.

4. The route is waymarked past the refreshment room here, almost immediately entering old oakwoods clothing the ravine cut by the River Doe. Steep steps reach a viewing opportunity to the foaming cauldron of **Beezley Falls**, from where the route now undulates like a big dipper, up and down countless steps and slopes. **Triple Spout** is a particularly vigorous set of falls, downstream from which the river slips into the immense, sheer chasm of **Baxenghyll Gorge**: for the confident

a thin footbridge is shot across this impressive gulch.

5. Snow Falls are the last of the show-falls; beyond here the path snakes through old quarry workings (look for orchids), presently reaching a tarred lane at the fringe of Ingleton. Follow the fingerposts through the village centre to return to the car park to complete the walk. ♦

Up in the air

The railway to Ingleton was built by two competing companies. The LNWR built southwards from Tebay and the Midland Railway northwards from Clapham, near Settle. Rivalry was so intense that, when completed in 1861, passengers couldn't cross the massive viaduct in a train, but had to walk between stations near either end. The arguments were only finally resolved by the building of the famous Settle and Carlisle Railway in 1875.

Late afternoon at the Linton Falls

Linton Falls

Explore the waterfalls and woodlands of Wharfedale around charming Grassington

What to expect:
Good paths, but often muddy by the river; one climb

Distance/time: 10km/ 6 miles. Allow 3 hours

Start/finish: National Park pay and display car park at Grassington

Grid ref: SE 003 637

Ordnance Survey Map: Explorer OL2 Yorkshire Dales: *Southern & Western areas: Whernside, Ingleborough & Pen-y-ghent*

After the walk: Plenty of cafés and pubs in Grassington

Walk outline

The River Wharfe sweeps below the quaint streets of Grassington, thundering over a series of limestone-step waterfalls at pretty Linton. From here paths continue upstream to the lively cataracts at Ghaistrill's Strid. The woodlands of Lower Grass Wood line the bank before tracks rise into the mixed fir and ashwoods above, emerging into a tranquil upland vale amidst great limestone scenery. The Dales Way is joined to return along paths and back-lanes to Grassington.

Limestone pavement

Grassington

Grassington stands beside the Wharfe at the foot of rippling moors that once hosted one of England's most intensive industrial landscapes. For centuries lead mining busied the local populace; today's charming village is unrecognisable from that of 130 years ago, when early tourists could visit the mines. The Wharfe's lively course amply repays a leisurely ramble, before threading up through magnificent woods to pass the site of the original village here. Lea Green's grassy jigsaw of mounds, tracks and circles dates from the Iron Age, when the Romans may have mined the nearby lodes of lead 2,000 years ago.

Kingfisher

The Walk

1. Walk along **Sedber Lane** cul-de-sac beside the car park, joining the path down to the **River Wharfe** and a footbridge across the waterfalls at **Linton**. The onward route is upstream to the right through the handgate here, signed for Grass Wood. Spend time, however, lingering above these contorted falls, dropping over natural limestone steps below the **Georgian Weir** which fed the village corn mill. Linton's appealing little Norman church is worth the detour—cross the footbridge to reach the village lane and turn left to find **St Michael & All Angels Church** in 500 metres.

2. Join the riverside path, keeping the water on your left. The modest building on the far bank at the higher weir is a power station.

Two water turbines were installed in 2011, replacing a similar scheme developed a century ago to supply electricity to Grassington. The new turbine house uses two Archimedean screws to work generators which can supply around 90 homes that power.

The well-worn path passes directly below the terrace of houses above Grassington's old bridge. Cross straight over the road (bad bend), rejoining the upstream path which threads beside haymeadows to reach **Ghaistrill's Strid**.

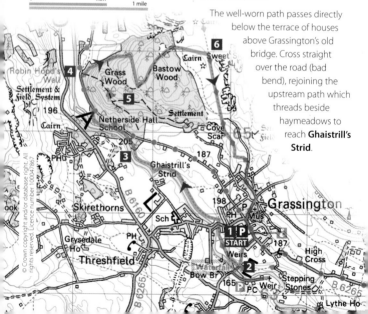

Little Linton: *The tiny Dales' village of Linton sits at the heart of a web of walls and barns*

Here the Wharfe has cleaved through beds of limestone, creating a long series of cataracts and shoots below low bluffs. It's a favourite spot for fly fishermen stalking brown trout; it's also a great place to chance upon dippers and wagtails hunting their insect prey above and below the torrents.

3. A little further upstream the path enters the fringe of **Lower Grass Wood**; the steep valley sides draped with ash, birch, oak and alder.

This is some of the most ancient woodland in the Yorkshire Dales; for centuries wood was burnt in stone-lined hearths here to produce potash, used as a soil improver.

The path rises steeply away from the river; then drops again before eventually bending right to reach a tarred lane, along which turn left.

4. Near the end of the woodland use the gate on your right to gain a wide track into **Grass Wood**; the fingerpost indicates 'Grassington 2 miles'. This gravelly track climbs easily within the edge of the woods; to your left views

Rock and river: *A long exposure transforms flowing water into silk*

north up the deep valley of Wharfedale focus on the distinctive snout of Kilnsey Crag, backed by the horseshoe of high fells enclosing the dale-head. Bend right with the main track, presently passing an open glade.

5. At the fingerposted cross-path turn left for 'Bastow Wood' (the path right, to 'Far Gregory', diverts to a wooded hilltop topped by an Iron Age hillfort). Cross the step-stile through the high bounding wall and keep ahead through scrubby **Bastow Wood**, the hummocky ground spangled in late spring with yellow rock rose. A ladder-stile leads to open country; go ahead on the grassy path away from the wall, soon walking through an area of **limestone pavement**. Sight the biggest tree ahead and pass just to its left, reaching a wide grassy path. *Scant remains here mark the original settlement from which Grassington much later developed.*

6. Turn right on this path, the **Dales Way**, with a wall to your left. The path presently crests, revealing a view to the line of Rylstone and Cracoe Fells, with Grassington in the near-distance. Take the lower route at a fork, looking in 150 metres for the fingerposted 'Dales Way'

stile. Beyond the next gap-stile drift left parallel to the lower, uneven wall, right, and passing above a large ash tree. Use the higher stile, heading then for the barns. Go left, as signed, over stiles across a field corner, continuing to the low stable block. Turn right on the walled lane; at the T-junction go left to Grassington Town Head. Turn right down to **The Square**; here go left to the car park to complete the walk. ◆

Wildlife wonderland

Grass Wood is gradually being cleared of 100-year old plantation trees and replaced by natural regeneration and broadleaf planting. The wood is renowned for its butterflies, including the northern brown argus, common- and holly blues. There's also a superb range of woodland wildflowers; the very rare rock-whitebeam tree, and a small number of roe deer.

Uldale Force

Uldale Force

A challenging approach to a remote series of falls secluded below Baugh Fell at the fringe of the Howgill Fells

What to expect:
Lanes, tracks and narrow paths; some scrambling; marshy sections

Distance/time: 10.5km/ 6½ miles; 3-4 hours

Start/finish: Layby beside A683 road 200 metres west of Rawthey Bridge, 6 miles north-east of Sedbergh

Grid ref: SD 712 978

Ordnance Survey Map: Explorer OL19 *Howgill Fells & Upper Eden Valley*

After the walk: The Cross Keys Temperance Inn at Cautley, 1 mile south of Rawthey Bridge; pubs, cafés and hotels in Sedbergh

Walk outline

This walk in the western fringe of the National Park follows a narrow lane across Ravenstonedale Common. A sparse quarrymen's path is joined up wooded Rawthey Gill, past a series of lively falls to reach the memorable downfall of Uldale Force. The return follows a reedy bridleway across the side of West Baugh Fell. Perversely, plan to do this walk after a good dry spell, as the paths near Uldale Force are thin and slippery.

Uldale Force

This seldom-visited corner of The Dales—actually in Cumbria—reveals a very unfamiliar countryside. The magnificent Howgill Fells create a memorable horizon. An astonishing series of waterfalls tumble from the heights into wooded gorges and gills, culminating in the matriarch of the system, the memorable Uldale Force, hidden in its remote canyon. Reaching it requires determination and surefootedness; the deceptively easy approach on tranquil lanes is soon replaced by thin, challenging paths etched into the gorge side.

This is the most demanding walk in this book; a richly rewarding exploration of an exquisite, hidden landscape.

White Green Farm

Nesting curlew

The Walk

1. Cross **Rawthey Bridge** and take the narrow lane forking right for 'Uldale Fell End'. This rises easily past a few remote farms, soon levelling along the edge of **Ravenstonedale Common**.

*To your left is a sweeping view of the Howgill Fells, described by the fellwalker Alfred Wainwright as 'looking like a herd of sleeping elephants'. The dark crags and screes are Cautley Crag, the flank of Great Dummacks. Along with adjoining Calf Fell, it is the highest land in these remote hills. Tumbling down the gash in the hillside here is **Cautley Spout**, England's highest waterfall which drops in stages over 180 metres.*

2. Turn right on the tarred lane signposted for 'Uldale Head', winding across rushy upland pasture that rises to the heights of looming **Wild Boar Fell**. *A few secluded farms dapple these acres; one at White Green is a poignant, abandoned reminder of times when far more people farmed these uplands.*

3. Where the lane forks, remain on the higher level, passing through a gate into **Uldale**, signed as a bridleway and footpath to 'Grisedale'. The concreted track dips through wooded **Needlehouse Gill**; at the far side, turn right on the fingerposted bridleway for 'Bluecaster', a pleasant wood-edged way carpeted with pinecones. Beyond a gate the track descends to cross a footbridge over the **River Rawthey**.

4. Turn upstream; the track soon deteriorates in quality and width. Roughly a kilometre later, just past a river-edge boulder fall, notice a two-metre high pillar of stones on a ledge up on your right; there are caverns behind. About 50 metres beyond, fork right, up the grassy path into old workings.

Cool waters: *The River Rawthey at Uldale*

Continue upstream, now perhaps 30 metres above the river. The thin path, vague in parts, presently crosses the clefts of two extremely steep gills. After the second, head downhill into the gorge, picking your way up to **Uldale Force**, secreted in a semicircular embayment.

5. Return to the footbridge. Don't cross it but instead join the stony track angling out of the valley. Remain with this for two kilometres across the flank of the moor, contrasting sharply with the grassy fields opposite.

6. At a lone, low bridleway marker turn right on a track back to **Rawthey Bridge** to complete the walk. ♦

Yorkshire Dales or Lake District?

The River Lune's gorge, which is followed by both the mainline railway and the M6, separates the Yorkshire Dales and Lake District National Parks. It was somehow overlooked when the Park designations were made in the 1950s. Today, this area of tortuous becks and remote fells—including the northern Howgills, Ravenstonedale, Wild Boar Fell and Great Asby Scar—is subject to draft legislation to bring it within the National Parks.

Hardraw Force

Hardraw Force

Find England's longest single-drop waterfall in the back garden of a fine Dales' pub

What to expect:
Tracks, lanes and field paths; marshy in places

Distance/time: 9.5km/ 6 miles. Allow 3 hours

Start/finish: Hawes National Park car park (pay & display)

Grid ref: SD 875 898

Ordnance Survey Map: Explorer OL30 Yorkshire Dales: *Northern & Central areas: Wensleydale & Swaledale*

After the walk: Teashops and inns in Hawes

Walk outline

From the Wensleydale market town of Hawes, the Pennine Way is joined, crossing the River Ure before striking through pasture to Hardraw hamlet. The sublime Hardraw Force is reached via the Green Dragon pub's back garden (fee payable) before tracks and field paths meander to Appersett. Join a lane beside the lively Widdale Beck, where smaller falls tumble near the old railway viaduct. Easy moorland roads and footpaths return to Hawes.

Hardraw Force

Hawes is renowned for its Wensleydale Cheese Creamery, which was famously revived by employees and locals following its corporate closure in 1992. The village is also situated near the meeting of half-a-dozen major and minor dales, the becks of which cascade down from the enclosing high fells over countless waterfalls.

River Ure roots

This walk visits the most famous of these falls, hidden in a gorge behind a sublime village pub; whilst others tumble prettily through village centres. Magnificent views of the northern Dales' accompany the walk, with stunning panoramas over this quiet corner of the National Park.

Brown hare

The Walk

1. From the eastern end of the town's one-way system near the **Ropemakers' Works**, take the road for 'Muker and Industrial Estate'. Look for a Pennine Way fingerpost here. Cross the former railway before slipping into the industrial estate road.

Look to the right for the **Pennine Way**, and follow it across fields to regain the road near **Haylands Bridge**. Cross this and, in another 200 metres, go left on the field path for 'Hardraw'. This well-walked path slinks across several pastures, rejoining the Pennine Way on the approach to **Hardraw** village and the nearby **Green Dragon Inn**.

The bar of this delightful pub is also the entrance to the waterfall! **Hardraw Force** is a thin dagger plummeting over 30 metres into a great limestone cove dripping with ferns and mosses. *The highest single-drop, overground falls in England, Hardraw was used as a location for the film* Robin Hood, Prince of Thieves. *The enchanting approach up a wooded chasm reveals a network of paths first developed by a Victorian entrepreneur. His 'improvements' included repairing the lip of the waterfall, which fell off in a violent storm-surge in 1899.*

2. Return from the falls, turn right from the inn and cross the bridge. Immediately past the **old school**, turn right on the **Pennine Way** up a walled track that curls above woodland.

White plume: *Hardraw Force plummets 30 metres into a vast limestone cove*

Magnificent views open out ahead to Great Shunner Fell, one of the highest points on the Pennine Way, whilst behind you is a grand panorama across higher Wensleydale.

Remain on the track as it levels out beyond the woods. Around 600 metres later, look for a gate on the left, signposted to 'New Bridge'.

3. Walk beside the wall down boggy pasture and cross a corner stile. The way now drops more steeply and slightly left, gaining the first of a line of wayposts guiding the route across rough pasture, heading just left of dome-topped Dodd Fell. Cross further stiles and aim well to the right of the **old barn** and sycamores to reach a road junction. Go left on the main Hawes road, cross the **New Bridge** over the **River Ure** and then slip right into a footpath parallel to the road. Stay with this to the bridge at the edge of **Appersett hamlet**.

4. Turn right off the bridge up the tarred lane, rising gently above **Widdale**

Green and pleasant land: *There are superb views over drystone-walled Wensleydale from the fells above Hardraw Force*

Beck. Noisy **waterfalls** mark its passage beneath the railway viaduct, a popular spot with abseilers. As the lane levels at a righthand-bend, take the path on the left, signposted to 'Ashes'. Head across the pasture on a faint track, go over a stone stile and drop through a shallow valley past a barn to a fingerpost near a ruinous lime kiln. Go right, through the higher handgate and then up the slope to a wall-gap. Turn hard-left, walking above the wall-line. Bend right with the field elbow, tracing the wall on your left to a gate into a lane.

5. Walk uphill to the nearby fork; then head along a rough track called **Cam Road**. In 400 metres, opposite a hut, turn left on another walled track and remain with this past farms to a T-junction.

6. Turn uphill to find the waymarked **Pennine Way**, signed to your left for 'West End'. Cross the hay meadows on a thin path through several handgates to another fingerpost. Take the path for 'Gayle', soon reaching a village lane. Turn right and wind through **Gayle** to the bridge over **Gayle Beck**. *Waterfalls*

cascade through the village and a leat leads to the nearby Victorian sawmill.

Turn back from the bridge and bend right for Hawes. At the slope-foot take the **Pennine Way** right, passing below

the creamery to reach **Hawes church**. Turn right on the path to the town centre where stepped waterfalls crash between the buildings, to complete the walk. ♦

Wensleydale cheese

Hawes was granted a market charter as late as 1699, replacing tiny Askrigg as the market centre for higher Wensleydale. The market thrived and continues to do so. Here, too, are the remarkable 200-year-old Ropemaker's Works, and the creamery where genuine Wensleydale cheese is produced. Even today it's still made using the original recipe first developed by monks at Jervaulx Abbey back in the 12th century.

Useful Information

'Welcome to Yorkshire'
This comprehensive website draws together a wealth of information about visiting Yorkshire. www.yorkshire.com

Yorkshire Dales National Park
For in-depth information about the National Park, including 'What's on' listings of local events and tourist information. www.yorkshiredales.org.uk

Visitor Centres
Many towns in the area have Tourist Information Centres where staff will help with accommodation, heritage and outdoor activities. The main ones are listed here; there are also National Park Centres in some key locations.

Tourist Information Centres
Horton-in-Ribblesdale	01729 860333	horton@ytbtic.co.uk
Ingleton	01524 241049	ingleton@ytbtic.co.uk
Leyburn	01748 828747	ticleyburn@richmondshire.co.uk
Sedbergh	01539 620125	tic@sedbergh.org.uk
Settle	01729 825192	settle@ytbtic.co.uk
Skipton	01756 792809	skipton@ytbtic.co.uk

National Park Centres
Open daily April-October; limited in winter; closed in January
Aysgarth Falls	01969 662910	aysgarth@yorkshiredales.org.uk
Grassington	01756 751690	grassington@yorkshiredales.org.uk
Hawes	01969 666210	hawes@yorkshiredales.org.uk
Malham	01969 652380	malham@yorkshiredales.org.uk
Reeth	01748 884059	reeth@yorkshiredales.org.uk

Emergencies
If you have an accident whilst out walking and are immobilised, call 112 on your mobile 'phone, ask for the police, and tell them to contact mountain rescue. Be ready to tell the operator your exact location (nearest village, plus features named on the map close to your location) and the nature of your injury.

Weather
For the latest report for the Yorkshire Dales follow the link on the National Park website (see above) for 'Weather'. For details of local weather, go to **www. mylocalweather.org.uk** and click on the area you're interested in.